CROCHET ESSENTIALS

Enjoy creativity, relaxation, and success—all at once—by crocheting these essential designs with Lion Brand® Yarn. These projects are great for anyone to create, but are especially suitable for beginners. That's because you only need to learn the basic stitches! You'll love the ease of extending your wardrobe with a scarf, neckwarmer, shrug, pocket market bag, and vest. Why not pamper the youngest member of the family with a matching cardigan and hat? Brighten your kitchen with our colorful collection of crocheted dishcloths. Add a warm and inviting touch to every room of your home with cozy afghans and a pillow. Don't forget your four-legged friends—the washable pet mats provide a warm place to rest. It's time to reward yourself (and your loved ones) with the beauty and comfort of Lion Brand Yarn!

HOMESPUN

GAUGE for 4"x 4" (10cm x 10cm) — 14 STS / 10 SC

	TOTAL	
	yards	meters
	185	169

ACRYLIC	POLYESTER
98%	2%

FANCY FUR

GAUGE for 4"x 4" (10cm x 10cm)

13	9mm	P-15	10mm
10 STS	12 R	6 SC	7 R

NET		TOTAL	
ozs	gms	yards	meters
1¾	50	39	35

POLYAMIDE	POLYESTER
55%	45%

FUN FUR

GAUGE for 4"x 4" (10cm x 10cm)

10.5	6.5mm	K-10.5	6.5mm
16 STS	20 R	12 SC	14 R

SOLIDS

NET		TOTAL	
ozs	gms	yards	meters
1¾	50	64	58

PRINTS

NET		TOTAL	
ozs	gms	yards	meters
1½	40	57	52

POLYESTER
100%

BABY SOFT

GAUGE for 4"x 4" (10cm x 10cm)

6	4mm	G-6	4mm
22 STS	30 R	16 SC	20 R

SOLIDS

NET		TOTAL	
ozs	gms	yards	meters
5	140	459	413

PRINTS

NET		TOTAL	
ozs	gms	yards	meters
4	112	367	330

ACRYLIC	NYLON
60%	40%

POMPADOUR

NET		TOTAL	
ozs	gms	yards	meters
4	112	367	330

ACRYLIC	NYLON	RAYON
62%	27%	11%

COTTON-EASE

GAUGE for 4"x 4" (10cm x 10cm)

8	5mm	H-8	5mm
17 STS	24 R	13.5 SC	15 R

NET		TOTAL	
ozs	gms	yards	meters
3½	100	207	188

ACRYLIC	COTTON
50%	50%

LION BOUCLÉ

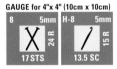

GAUGE for 4"x 4" (10cm x 10cm)

11	8mm	N-13	9mm
10 STS	14 R	8 SC	7 R

NET		TOTAL	
ozs	gms	yards	meters
2½	70	57	52

ACRYLIC	MOHAIR	NYLON
79%	20%	1%

LION COTTON

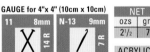

GAUGE for 4"x 4" (10cm x 10cm)

7	4.5mm	F-5	3.75mm
16 STS	24 R	16 SC	16 R

SOLIDS

NET		TOTAL	
ozs	gms	yards	meters
5	140	236	212

PRINTS

NET		TOTAL	
ozs	gms	yards	meters
4	112	189	170

COTTON
100%

JIFFY

GAUGE for 4"x 4" (10cm x 10cm)

10	6mm	K-10.5	6.5mm
14.6 STS	18 R	10 SC	12 R

SOLIDS

NET		TOTAL	
ozs	gms	yards	meters
3	85	135	123

HEATHER BLUE & PRINTS

NET		TOTAL	
ozs	gms	yards	meters
2½	70	115	103

ACRYLIC
100%

WOOL-EASE

GAUGE for 4"x 4" (10cm x 10cm)

8	5mm	J-10	6mm
18 STS	24 R	13.2 SC	16 R

SOLIDS, HEATHERS, & TWISTS

NET		TOTAL	
ozs	gms	yards	meters
3	85	197	180

WOOL	ACRYLIC
20%	80%

SPRINKLES, WHEAT, & MUSHROOM

NET		TOTAL	
ozs	gms	yards	meters
3	85	197	180

WOOL	ACRYLIC	RAYON
10%	86%	4%

MULTICOLORS

NET		TOTAL	
ozs	gms	yards	meters
2½	70	162	146

WOOL	ACRYLIC	POLYESTER
19%	78%	3%

PRINTS

NET		TOTAL	
ozs	gms	yards	meters
2½	70	162	146

WOOL	ACRYLIC
20%	80%

FROSTS

NET		TOTAL	
ozs	gms	yards	meters
2½	70	162	146

WOOL	ACRYLIC	POLYESTER
20%	70%	10%

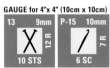
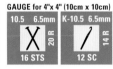
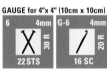

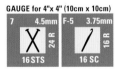
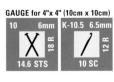

LEARN TO CROCHET

Just follow these basic steps and you'll be crocheting in no time at all!

■ CROCHETING IS FUN AND CREATIVE

Crocheting will give you years of enjoyment. The repetitive nature of crochet is a proven stress reducer. Plus, the variety of stitches, patterns and materials available to crocheters makes crocheting a wonderful outlet for your creativity. So, whether you're looking to add the latest fashions to your wardrobe or dress up your home in style, crocheting will fit into your lifestyle.

■ BEFORE YOU START

Find a comfortable chair in good light. Read through the steps before you begin. As with any new skill, learning to crochet requires equal measures of patience and perseverance. Remember, crocheting should be a fun experience. If you get stuck, take a deep breath to relax, but keep at it.

■ GETTING A GRIP

Crochet is a method of creating fabric from yarn or thread, by using a hook and a ball of yarn. The hook is generally held in the right hand as shown. Even lefties can learn to crochet this way or they can reverse the instructions. There are two basic "holds". Use whichever method feels more comfortable to you.

In the first method, you hold the hook as you would a pencil, grasping the hook between your thumb and index finger (**Fig. 1**).

Fig. 1

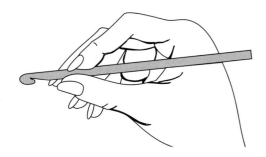

In the knife method, place your right hand over the hook and grasp it between your thumb and index finger to begin (**Fig. 2**). The left hand is used to control the yarn and to hold the stitches as they are created.

Fig. 2

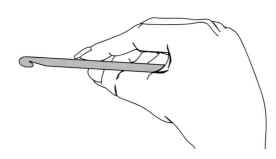

■ LET'S START AT THE BEGINNING

To begin, you'll need to make the first loop on your hook, a slip knot.

Pull the yarn strand from the center of the ball. Make a loop shape 5" or 6" from the end (the tail) by placing the tail in front of the ball yarn, then letting the rest of the tail yarn fall slightly behind the loop.

Insert your hook into the loop (**Fig. 3**). Scoop up the yarn in the back of the loop with the hook. Pull through the front of the loop. Gently pull the tail yarn to tighten loop around the hook. In crocheting, the slip knot does not count as a stitch.

Fig. 3

■ MAKING A CHAIN STITCH (abbreviated as ch)

Hold the hook in your right hand and loop the yarn from the ball over your left index finger. Hold the end of the slip knot between the thumb and middle finger of your left hand. With your left index finger, wrap the yarn from back to front around the shaft of the hook (**Fig. 4**). Use the hook to draw the yarn through the loop on the hook – one chain is now made.

Fig. 4

Make as many chains as your pattern calls for (**Fig. 5**). The resulting row of chains is called the foundation chain. You will build the crocheted fabric off of this foundation. The chain stitch is also used to produce spaces and loops in your fabric.

Fig. 5

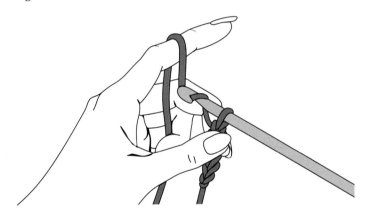

■ ALL ABOUT STITCHES

The illustration below shows how to count the chain stitches you have worked (**Fig. 6**). When counting chains, do not include the slip knot at the end or the loop on your hook as a stitch.

Fig. 6

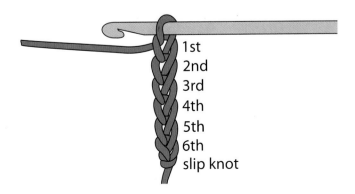

1st
2nd
3rd
4th
5th
6th
slip knot

Each crochet stitch has 2 loops on the top of the stitch. The illustration below identifies these loops (**Fig. 7**). Usually, you will insert your hook under both loops of the stitch in the previous row. Sometimes, to create a decorative effect, a pattern will indicate to work in either the front loop or back loop of a stitch.

Fig. 7

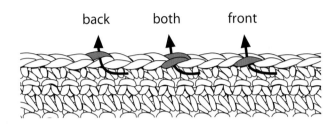

back   both   front

■ TURNING CHAINS

Stitches in crochet come in varying heights. When you begin a row of any stitch, you will be starting at the base of the row. In order to come up to the height of the stitch you will be working, you must start with a chain that is the same height as the stitches in the row you are working. This chain is called the turning chain. It can be worked before or after turning your work. The illustration below shows the most common stitches and the length of the turning chain for each stitch (**Fig. 8**).

Fig. 8

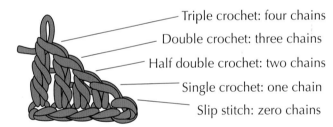

— Triple crochet: four chains
— Double crochet: three chains
— Half double crochet: two chains
— Single crochet: one chain
— Slip stitch: zero chains

Usually, the turning chain at the beginning of the row, takes the place of the first stitch of the row. So, after working the turning chain, you will not work another stitch in the first stitch. And when you come to the end of the row, you will treat the turning chain as a stitch and work in it. For the single crochet, the rules change. The turning chain worked at the beginning of a single crochet row does not count as a stitch. After working the turning chain, you will also work a single crochet in the stitch below the turning chain. You will not work in the turning chain on the return row.

■ TURNING YOUR WORK

When you come to the end of a row, the instructions will tell you to turn your work. Refer to the illustration below (**Fig. 9**).

Fig. 9

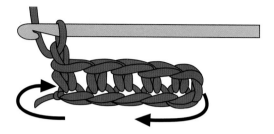

Simply rotate your crochet piece, clockwise halfway around so that the last stitch you worked now becomes the first stitch in the row below (**Fig. 10**).

Fig. 10

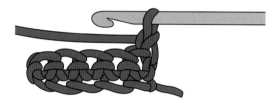

■ MAKING A SINGLE CROCHET (abbreviated sc)

The single crochet is the most basic crochet stitch for making fabric. All the other stitches are variations on this one.

Make a foundation chain one chain more than the number of single crochet stitches called for. Insert hook from front to back in the center of the second chain from the hook (**Fig. 11**).

Fig. 11

Wrap the yarn, from back to front, around the hook (this is called yarn over and is abbreviated yo), draw the yarn through the chain (2 loops on hook) (**Fig. 12**).

Fig. 12

Yarn over, draw through 2 loops on hook (one single crochet complete) (**Fig. 13**).

Fig. 13

Insert hook in the center of next chain, yarn over, draw yarn through stitch, yarn over, draw yarn through 2 loops on hook. Repeat across to end of foundation chain.

To begin the second row, chain one for the turning chain (does not count as a stitch) (**Fig. 14**). Turn your work (**Fig. 15**).

Fig. 14

turning chain →

Fig. 15

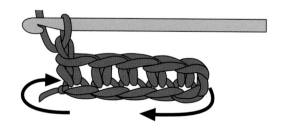

Insert hook from front to back under the top 2 loops of the first single crochet in the row below (**Fig. 16**), yarn over, draw yarn through stitch, yarn over, draw yarn through 2 loops on hook (first single crochet complete). Repeat this step in each single crochet across (**Fig. 17**).

Fig. 16

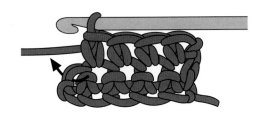

Fig. 17

■ MAKING A HALF DOUBLE CROCHET (abbreviated hdc)

The half double crochet comes halfway between a single crochet and a double crochet in height.

Make a foundation chain one chain more than the number of half double crochet stitches called for. Skip first 2 chain stitches (will count as the turning chain). Yarn over hook once, insert hook from front to back in the center of the third chain from the hook (**Fig. 18**).

Fig. 18

Yarn over, draw the yarn through the chain (3 loops on hook) (**Fig. 19**).

Fig. 19

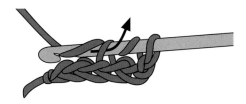

Yarn over, draw through 3 loops on hook (**Fig. 20**) (one half double crochet complete) (**Fig. 21**).

Fig. 20

Fig. 21

Yarn over, insert hook in the center of next chain, yarn over, draw yarn through stitch, yarn over, draw yarn through 3 loops on hook. Repeat across to end of foundation chain.

To begin the second row, turn your work. Chain two for the turning chain (**Fig. 22**).

Fig. 22

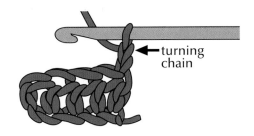
turning chain

Skip the first half double crochet below the turning chain. Yarn over, insert hook from front to back under the top 2 loops of the next half double crochet in the row below (**Fig. 23**), yarn over, draw yarn through stitch, yarn over, draw yarn through 3 loops on hook (half double crochet complete). Repeat this step in each half double crochet across and in the top of the beginning chain at the end of the row (**Fig. 24**).

Fig. 23

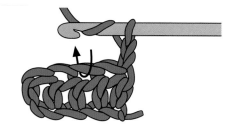

Fig. 24

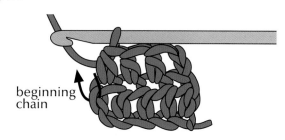

beginning chain

■ MAKING A DOUBLE CROCHET (abbreviated dc)

The double crochet is about twice the height of a single crochet. It is a very popular stitch producing a looser fabric than single crochet.

Make foundation chain 2 chains more than the number of double crochet stitches called for. Skip first 3 chain stitches (will count as the turning chain).

Yarn over hook once, insert hook from front to back in the center of the fourth chain from the hook (**Fig. 25**).

Fig. 25

Yarn over, draw the yarn through the chain (3 loops on hook) (**Fig. 26**).

Fig. 26

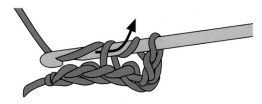

Yarn over, draw yarn through 2 loops on hook (2 loops remain on hook) (**Fig. 27**).

Fig. 27

Yarn over, draw through 2 loops on hook (**Fig. 28**) (one double crochet complete) (**Fig. 29**).

Fig. 28

Fig. 29

Yarn over, insert hook in the center of next chain, yarn over, draw yarn through stitch, yarn over, draw yarn through 2 loops on hook, yarn over, draw yarn through 2 loops on hook. Repeat across to end of foundation chain.

To begin the second row, turn your work. Chain three for the turning chain (**Fig. 30**).

Fig. 30

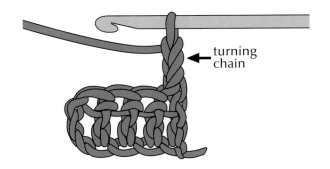

Skip the first double crochet below the turning chain. Yarn over, insert hook from front to back under the top 2 loops of the next double crochet in the row below (**Fig. 31**), yarn over, draw yarn through stitch, yarn over, draw yarn through 2 loops on hook, yarn over, draw yarn through 2 loops on hook (double crochet complete). Repeat this step in each double crochet across and in the top of the beginning chain at the end of the row (**Fig. 32**).

Fig. 31

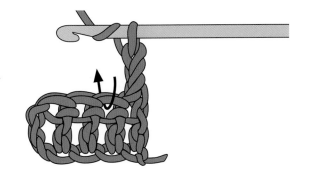

Fig. 32

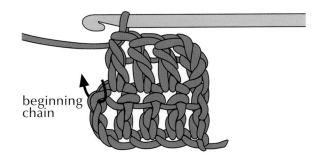

■ MAKING A TREBLE CROCHET (abbreviated trc)

The triple crochet is a little taller than a double crochet.

Make foundation chain 3 chains more than the number of triple crochet stitches called for. Skip first 4 chain stitches (will count as the turning chain). Yarn over hook (twice), insert hook from front to back in the center of the fifth chain from the hook (**Fig. 33**).

Fig. 33

Yarn over, draw the yarn through the chain (3 loops on hook) (**Fig. 34**).

Fig. 34

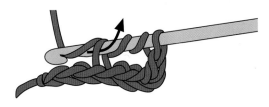

Yarn over, draw yarn through 2 loops on hook (3 loops remain on hook) (**Fig. 35**).

Fig. 35

Yarn over, draw yarn through 2 loops on hook (2 loops remain on hook) (**Fig. 36**).

Fig. 36

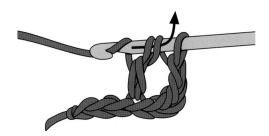

Yarn over, draw through 2 loops on hook (**Fig. 37**) (one triple crochet complete) (**Fig. 38**).

Fig. 37

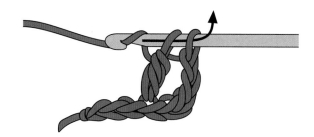

Fig. 38

Yarn over (twice), insert hook in the center of next chain, yarn over, draw yarn through stitch, [yarn over, draw yarn through 2 loops on hook] 3 times. Repeat across to end of foundation chain.

To begin the second row, turn your work. Chain four for the turning chain (**Fig. 39**).

Fig. 39

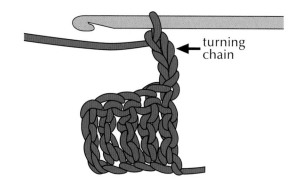

turning chain

Skip the first triple crochet below the turning chain. Yarn over (twice), insert hook from front to back under the top 2 loops of the next triple crochet in the row below (**Fig. 40**), [yarn over, draw yarn through 2 loops on] 3 times (first triple crochet complete). Repeat this step in each triple crochet across and in the top of the beginning chain at the end of the row (**Fig. 41**).

Fig. 40

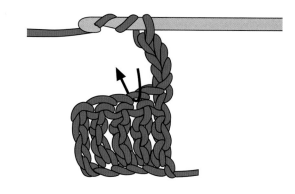

Fig. 41

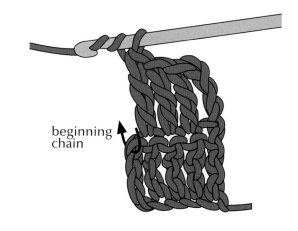

beginning chain

■ MAKING A SLIP STITCH (abbreviated sl st)

A slip stitch has very little height. It is used to join stitches that are worked in rounds such as a granny square. It is also used to travel to another part of a row without producing any visible stitches (such as indenting an armhole on a sweater).

To work a slip stitch into a chain stitch, first make a foundation chain of desired length, insert hook in last chain of foundation chain.

Yarn over, draw yarn through chain and the loop on your hook in one motion (slip stitch made) (**Fig. 42**).

Fig. 42

To work a slip stitch in a row stitches (single crochet stitches pictured), insert hook under the top 2 loops of the next stitch, yarn over, draw yarn through stitch and the loop on your hook in one motion (slip stitch made) (**Fig. 43**).

Fig. 43

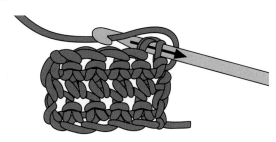

■ FASTENING OFF

When you finish a piece of crocheted fabric, you'll need to fasten off the yarn and secure it so the stitch will not unravel. Simply cut the yarn leaving a few inches of tail. Then, with your hook, draw the tail through the loop on your hook (**Fig. 44**). Remove hook and pull on tail to tighten. With a yarn needle, weave the tail through the stitches of the fabric to hide it.

Fig. 44

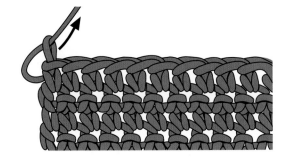

■ SEAMING TECHNIQUES

When you crochet a project in one piece such as a scarf, no seaming is required. But, some projects are made of several pieces that need to be joined together to form the finished piece.

The simplest method to join two pieces is to sew them. This produces a non-bulky seam, suitable for garments.

Working a row of slip stitches or single crochet produces a sturdy seam suitable for joining afghan squares. Worked on the right side, these two methods produce a decorative ridge that can be a nice addition.

INVISIBLE SEWN SEAM

Place the 2 pieces right sides facing up (that's the side you want to show), next to each other, matching stitches across the side edges.

Thread needle with a length of yarn. With the needle, weave the yarn though the stitches on one piece, bringing needle out at the corner to begin sewing. Leave a few inches of yarn woven through fabric to secure. Do not make a knot.

Insert needle through the corner of opposite piece and draw yarn through.

Insert needle through next row-end stitch on the first piece and draw yarn through.

Continue to sew up the seam, working in a zigzag pattern for the length of the seam (**Fig. 45**). Weave yarn through several stitches to anchor it, then cut tail.

Fig. 45

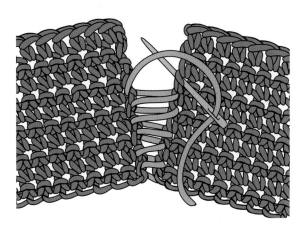

SLIP STITCH SEAM

Align two pieces, with right sides facing each other, matching stitches to be joined.

Make a slip knot on your yarn. Insert hook through first stitch of both pieces, draw through slip stitch, insert hook through next stitch of both pieces, yarn over, draw yarn through both stitches and loop on hook, in one motion.

Continue across edge to complete seam (**Fig. 46**). Fasten off.

Fig. 46

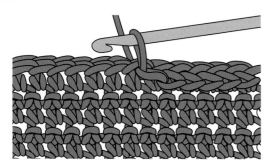

SINGLE CROCHET SEAM

A single crochet seam is worked in the same manner as the slip stitch seam, by substituting single crochet stitches for the slip stitches (**Fig 47**).

Fig. 47

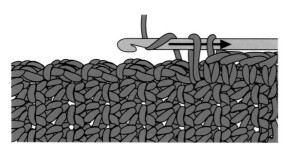

■ GAUGE

Gauge is the term that is used to define the proper tension you should work to insure that the crocheted piece you make will be the right size when it's completed. The hook size listed in the pattern is just the size used by the designer to work at the proper gauge. You may need to change hook size in order to work at the given gauge. It is especially important to work to the proper gauge when making garments – anything that you want to fit properly.

Gauge is usually defined in the pattern by a ratio of stitches and rows to a given measurement such as 16 stitches and 14 rows in single crochet = 4". You should always work a swatch of fabric (approximately 4" x 4") in the stitch pattern of the piece you are making. Then count the number of stitches and rows in the measurement designated by the gauge given in the pattern. If you find that your swatch has more stitches and rows than the gauge, you are working too tightly so change to a larger hook and try again. If you have fewer stitches and rows in the area, you are working too loosely and should try a smaller hook. Keep changing hook size until you arrive at the proper gauge.

■ JOINING A NEW BALL OF YARN

Sooner or later you are going to run out of yarn. It's best to join the new ball at the end of a row for a neater appearance. When you're about to run out of yarn, work your last stitch until there are 2 loops left on your hook. Leaving a tail, draw the end of the new yarn through the 2 loops on your hook. Then continue working with the new ball of yarn (**Fig. 48**). With a large-eyed needle, weave in the tails of both balls of yarn to secure. This method is also used when joining a new color of yarn.

Fig. 48

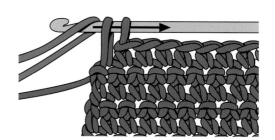

OTHER ABBREVIATIONS AND INFORMATION

■ ■

beg = begin(ning)
ch = chain
ch-sp = space previously made
dc = double crochet
hdc = half double crochet
inc = increas(e)(s)(ing)
rep = repeat
rnd = round
sc = single crochet
sk = skip
sl = slip
st(s) = stitch(es)
t-ch = turning chain

( ) or [ ] — work enclosed instructions **as many** times as specified by the number immediately following **or** contains explanatory remarks.
colon (:) — the number(s) given after a colon at the end of a row or round denote(s) the number of stitches or spaces you should have on that row or round.

CROCHET TERMINOLOGY	
UNITED STATES	**INTERNATIONAL**
slip stitch (slip st) =	single crochet (sc)
single crochet (sc) =	double crochet (dc)
half double crochet (hdc) =	half treble crochet (htr)
double crochet (dc) =	treble crochet (tr)
treble crochet (tr) =	double treble crochet (dtr)
double treble crochet (dtr) =	triple treble crochet (ttr)
triple treble crochet (tr tr) =	quadruple treble crochet (qtr)
skip =	miss

Yarn Weight Symbol & Names	SUPER FINE 1	FINE 2	LIGHT 3	MEDIUM 4	BULKY 5	SUPER BULKY 6
Type of Yarns in Category	Sock, Fingering Baby	Sport, Baby	DK, Light Worsted	Worsted, Afghan, Aran	Chunky, Craft, Rug	Bulky, Roving
Crochet Gauge Ranges in Single Crochet to 4" (10 cm)	21-32 sts	16-20 sts	12-17 sts	11-14 sts	8-11 sts	5-9 sts
Advised Hook Size Range	B-1 to E-4	E-4 to 7	7 to I-9	I-9 to K-10.5	K-10.5 to M-13	M-13 and larger

CROCHET HOOKS												
U.S.	B-1	C-2	D-3	E-4	F-5	G-6	H-8	I-9	J-10	K-10½	N	P	Q
Metric - mm	2.25	2.75	3.25	3.5	3.75	4	5	5.5	6	6.5	9	10	15

●□□□ **BEGINNER**		Projects for first-time crocheters using basic stitches. Minimal shaping.
●●□□ **EASY**		Projects using yarn with basic stitches, repetitive stitch patterns, simple color changes, and simple shaping and finishing.
●●●□ **INTERMEDIATE**		Projects using a variety of techniques, such as basic lace patterns or color patterns, mid-level shaping and finishing.
●●●● **EXPERIENCED**		Projects with intricate stitch patterns, techniques and dimension, such as non-repeating patterns, multi-color techniques, fine threads, small hooks, detailed shaping and refined finishing.

BABY CARDIGAN AND HAT

DESIGNER: **MOLLY BETTRIDGE**

 **EASY**

Finished Sizes: 9 months (18 months, 3 years)
Finished Chest: 24 (27, 30)" [61 (68.5, 76) cm]
Finished Length: 12½ (13½, 15)" [32 (34.5, 38) cm]
Finished Hat Circumference: 18" [45.5 cm]

Note: Cardigan pattern is written for smallest size with changes for larger sizes in parentheses. When only one number is given, it applies to all sizes. To follow pattern more easily, circle all numbers pertaining to your size before beginning.

MATERIALS

LION BRAND® Wool-Ease® **MEDIUM 4**
  Worsted Weight Yarn [3 ounces, 197 yards
  (85 grams, 180 meters) per ball]
  3 (3, 4) balls #188 Paprika (A)
  1 ball #171 Gold (B)
  or colors of your choice
LION BRAND crochet hook size I-9 [5.5 mm]
  or size needed for gauge
LION BRAND large-eyed blunt needle
LION BRAND stitch markers
LION BRAND pom-pom maker
Three ¾" [20 mm] buttons

GAUGE
12 hdc and 8 rows = 4" [10 cm]

■ CARDIGAN
■ BACK
With A, ch 38 (41, 44).

Row 1: Hdc in 3rd ch from hook and in each ch across: 36 (39, 42) hdc.

Row 2: Ch 2, turn, hdc in each st across.

Repeat Row 2 until piece measures 12½ (13½, 15)" [32 (34.5, 38) cm] from beg. Fasten off.

■ FRONT
(make 2)
With A, ch 21 (24, 27).

Row 1: Hdc in 3rd ch from hook and in each ch across: 19 (22, 25) hdc.

Row 2: Ch 2, turn, hdc in each st across.

Repeat Row 2 until piece measures same as Back. Fasten off.

■ SLEEVES
(make 2)
With A, ch 20 (20, 22).

Row 1: Hdc in 3rd ch from hook and in each ch across: 18 (18, 20) hdc.

Row 2: Ch 2, turn, hdc in each st across.

Row 3 (inc row)**:** Ch 2, turn, 2 hdc in first hdc (inc made), hdc in each hdc across to last hdc, 2 hdc in last hdc: 20 (20, 22) sts.

Rows 4-13 (17, 17): Repeat last 2 rows 5 (7, 7) times: 30 (34, 36) hdc.

Repeat Row 2 until piece measures 8½ (9½, 10½)" [21.5 (24, 26.5) cm] from beg. Fasten off.

■ FINISHING
Sew Fronts and Back together for 3¼" [8.5 cm] on each side for shoulders. Mark 5 (5½, 6)" [12.5 (14, 15) cm] down from shoulders on Fronts and Back for Sleeve placement. Sew tops of Sleeves between markers. Sew side and Sleeve seams.

Edging
From right side, join A with sl st in a side seam on lower edge; ch 1, work 1 round sc evenly spaced around Back, Fronts and neck, working 3 sc at each corner. Join with sl st in beg ch, fasten off.

Turn up cuffs. Fold down lapels and sew in place. Sew on buttons. Weave in ends.

■ HAT

With A, ch 56.

Row 1: Hdc in 3rd ch from hook and in each ch across: 54 hdc.

Row 2: Ch 2, turn, hdc in each st across.

Repeat Row 2 until piece measures 6" [15 cm] from beg. Fasten off.

■ FINISHING

Fold Hat in half, bringing side edges together, so it measures 9" x 6" [23 x 15 cm]. Sew together along side edge and one end. From wrong side, tack both corners at top of Hat together.

Pom-Pom

With 1 strand each of A and B, and following package directions, make a 2" [5 cm] Pom-pom. Sew Pom-pom to top of Hat. Weave in ends.

STRIPED SCARF

DESIGNER: **ANNEMARIE LAWSON**

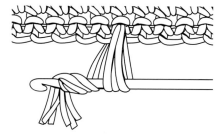

Fig.1

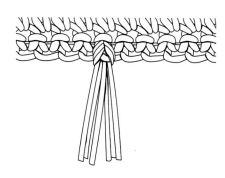

■ ◉▢▢▢ BEGINNER

Finished Size: 6" x 66" [15 x 167.5 cm]

MATERIALS

LION BRAND® Wool-Ease® **4** MEDIUM

    Worsted Weight Yarn [3 ounces, 197 yards
    (85 grams, 180 meters) per ball]
    2 balls #195 Azalea Pink (A)
    1 ball #188 Paprika (B)
    or colors of your choice
LION BRAND crochet hook size J-10 [6 mm]
    or size needed for gauge
LION BRAND large-eyed blunt needle
7" [18 cm] piece of heavy cardboard

GAUGE

11 half double crochet and 12 rows = 4" [10 cm]

Note: To change color, work last half double crochet to the point where there are 3 loops on hook; yarn over with new color to complete half double crochet.

■ SCARF

With A, chain 182.

Row 1: Half double crochet in 3rd chain from hook and in each chain across: 180 half double crochet.

Row 2: With A, chain 2, turn, half double crochet in each half double crochet across; change to B in last stitch.

Row 3: With B, repeat Row 2; change to A in last stitch.

Rows 4 and 5: With A, repeat Row 2; change to B in last stitch of Row 5.

Repeat Rows 3-5 four more times. Do not change to B in last stitch of last row. Fasten off.

■ FINISHING

Weave in ends.

Fringe

Cut 120 strands of A and 100 strands of B, each about 14" [35.5 cm] long. For each Fringe, hold 10 strands of yarn together and fold in half. Use crochet hook to draw fold through edge of Scarf, forming a loop. Pull ends of Fringe through this loop (**Fig. 1**). Pull to tighten (**Fig. 2**). Make 6 A and 5 B Fringes along each end of Scarf. Trim Fringe evenly.

Fig. 2

RECTANGLE VEST

DESIGNER: **K.J. HAY**

 BEGINNER

Finished Sizes: S (M, L, 1X, 2X)
Finished Bust: 36 (40, 44, 48, 52)" [91.5 (101.5, 112, 122, 132) cm]
Finished Length: 21 (21½, 22, 22½, 23)" [53.5 (54.5, 56, 57, 58.5) cm]

Note: Pattern is written for smallest size with changes for larger sizes in parentheses. When only one number is given, it applies to all sizes. To follow pattern more easily, circle all numbers pertaining to your size before beginning.

MATERIALS

LION BRAND® Wool-Ease® [MEDIUM 4]
  Worsted Weight Yarn [3 ounces, 197 yards (85 grams, 180 meters) per ball]
  4 balls #174 Avocado
  or color of your choice
LION BRAND crochet hook size J-10 [6 mm]
  or size needed for gauge
LION BRAND large-eyed blunt needle

GAUGE

12 stitches and 10 rows = 4" [10 cm] in pattern

Note: Back and Fronts are crocheted sideways.

■ BACK

Chain 64 (66, 67, 69, 70).

Row 1: Single crochet in 2nd chain from hook and in each chain across: 63 (65, 66, 68, 69) single crochet.

Row 2: Chain 3 (counts as first double crochet), turn, double crochet in next single crochet and in each single crochet across: 63 (65, 66, 68, 69) double crochet.

Row 3: Chain 1, turn, single crochet in each double crochet across.

Repeat Rows 2 and 3 until piece measures 18 (20, 22, 24, 26)" [45.5 (51, 56, 61, 66) cm] from beginning. Fasten off.

■ FRONT
(make 2)
Work as for Back until piece measures 8 (9, 10, 11, 12)" [20.5 (23, 25.5, 28, 30.5) cm] from beginning. Fasten off.

■ FINISHING

Sew shoulder seams. Beginning at lower edge, sew 12½ (13, 13, 13½, 13½)" [32 (33, 33, 34.5, 34.5) cm] side seams. Leave 8½ (8½, 9, 9, 9½)" [21.5 (21.5, 23, 23, 24) cm] open for armholes.

■ BELT

Chain 163.

Row 1: Single crochet in 2nd chain from hook and in each chain across.

Rows 4-9: Repeat Rows 2 and 3 of Back.

Fasten off. Weave in ends.

GRANNY SQUARE PILLOW

DESIGNER: **SHARON SILVERMAN**

 **EASY**

Finished Size: 14" [35.5 cm] square

MATERIALS
LION BRAND® Jiffy® **BULKY 5**
 Bulky Weight Yarn [3 ounces, 135 yards
 (85 grams, 123 meters) per ball]
 1 ball #122 Caffé (A)
 1 ball #115 Chili (B)
 or colors of your choice
LION BRAND crochet hook size H-8 [5 mm]
 or size needed for gauge
LION BRAND large-eyed blunt needle
Pillow form 14" [35.5 cm]

GAUGE
13 dc and 4½ rounds = 4" [10 cm]
One granny square = 7" [18 cm]

■ GRANNY SQUARE
(make 4 with A, 4 with B)

Ch 6; join with sl st in first ch to form a ring.

Rnd 1: Ch 3 (counts as dc here and throughout), 2 dc in ring, ch 1, (3 dc in ring, ch 1) 3 times; join with sl st in top of beg ch.

Rnd 2: Ch 3, dc in next 2 sts, *(2 dc, ch 1, 2 dc) in ch-sp (corner made), dc in next 3 sts; rep from * 2 more times, (2 dc, ch 1, 2 dc) in last ch-sp (corner made); join with sl st in top of beg ch.

Rnd 3: Ch 3, *dc in each dc to corner ch-sp, (2 dc, ch 1, 2 dc) in corner ch-sp; rep from * 3 more times, dc in each dc to end of rnd; join with sl st in top of beg ch.

Rnds 4 and 5: Rep Rnd 3. Fasten off. Weave in ends.

■ PILLOW
■ FRONT
Alternating A and B, arrange 4 squares in checkerboard fashion. Sew squares together to make Pillow Front.

■ BACK
Make same as Front.

■ FINISHING
Place Front and Back together, right sides facing out. Sc evenly around 3 sides through both layers to join. Do not fasten off. Insert pillow form. Sc evenly across last side; join with sl st in first sc. Fasten off. Weave in ends.

Assembly Diagram

A	B
B	A

GRANNY SQUARE AFGHAN

DESIGNER: **SHARON SILVERMAN**

 **EASY**

Finished Size: 39" x 59" [99 x 150 cm]

MATERIALS
LION BRAND® Jiffy® **BULKY 5**
 Bulky Weight Yarn [3 ounces, 135 yards
 (85 grams, 123 meters) per ball]
 6 balls #122 Caffé (A)
 4 balls #115 Chili (B)
 or colors of your choice
LION BRAND crochet hook size H-8 [5 mm]
 or size needed for gauge
LION BRAND large-eyed blunt needle

GAUGE
One granny square = 7" [18 cm]

■ GRANNY SQUARE
(make 24 with A, 15 with B)

Ch 6; join with sl st in first ch to form a ring.

Rnd 1: Ch 3 (counts as dc here and throughout), 2 dc in ring, ch 1, (3 dc in ring, ch 1) 3 times; join with sl st in top of beg ch.

Rnd 2: Ch 3, dc in next 2 sts, *(2 dc, ch 1, 2 dc) in ch-sp (corner made), dc in next 3 sts; rep from * 2 more times, (2 dc, ch 1, 2 dc) in last ch-sp (corner made); join with sl st in top of beg ch.

Rnd 3: Ch 3, *dc in each dc to corner ch-sp, (2 dc, ch 1, 2 dc) in corner ch-sp; rep from * 3 more times, dc in each dc to end of rnd; join with sl st in top of beg ch.

Rnds 4 and 5: Rep Rnd 3. Fasten off.

■ AFGHAN
Sew squares together following Assembly diagram.

■ FINISHING
Weave in ends.

Assemby Diagram

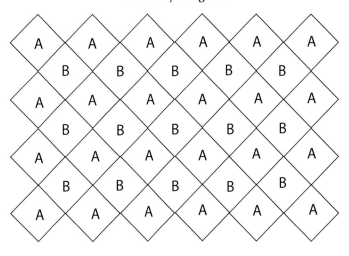

RIPPLE AFGHAN

DESIGNER: **CINDY GROSCH**

■ ◖■□□ **EASY**

Finished Size: 40" x 50" [101.5 x 127 cm]

MATERIALS
LION BRAND® Jiffy®
  Bulky Weight Yarn [3 ounces, 135 yards
  (85 grams, 123 meters) per ball]
  4 balls #134 Avocado (A)
  2 balls #132 Apple Green (B)
  or colors of your choice
LION BRAND® Wool-Ease®
  Worsted Weight Yarn [3 ounces, 197 yards
  (85 grams, 180 meters) per ball]
  3 balls #174 Avocado (C)
  or color of your choice
LION BRAND Crochet hook size L-11 [8 mm]
  or size needed for gauge
LION BRAND large-eyed blunt needle

GAUGE
13 sts = 4" [10 cm]

Note: To change color, work last stitch to the point where there are 2 loops on hook, yarn over with new color to complete stitch.

■ AFGHAN
With A, ch 134.

Row 1: Sc in 2nd ch from hook and in next 5 ch, 3 sc in next ch, sc in next 6 ch, *sk 2 ch, sc in next 6 ch, 3 sc in next ch, sc in next 6 ch; rep from * across: 135 sc.

Row 2: Ch 1, turn, sc in first sc, sk next sc, sc in next 5 sc, 3 sc in next sc, *sc in next 6 sc, sk 2 sc, sc in next 6 sc, 3 sc in next sc; rep from * to last 7 sc, sc in next 5 sc, sk next sc, sc in last sc.

Rows 3 and 4: Rep Row 2; change to B in last st.

Row 5: With B, rep Row 2; change to C in last st.

Rows 6 and 7: With C, rep Row 2; change to B in last st.

Row 8: With B, rep Row 2; change to A in last st.

Row 9: With A, rep Row 2.

Rep Rows 2-9 maintaining color sequence (4 rows A, 1 row B, 2 rows C, 1 row B), until Afghan measures 50" [127 cm] from beginning. Fasten off.

■ FINISHING
Edging: From RS, join C, ready to work across one Ripple end of Afghan. *Rep Row 2 across end, work 2 sc in corner, 140 sc along side of Afghan, rep from *. Sl st in beg st to join.

Next Rnd: *Rep Row 2 across end, work 2 sc in corner, sc in each st along side of Afghan, rep from *. Sl st in beg st to join.

Rep last rnd once. Fasten off.

Weave in ends.

CAT MAT

 EASY

Finished Size: 15" x 19" [38 x 48.5 cm]

MATERIALS

LION BRAND® Wool-Ease®
Worsted Weight Yarn [3 ounces, 197 yards
(85 grams, 180 meters) per ball]
1 ball #195 Azalea Pink (A)
1 ball #146 Lilac (C)
or colors of your choice
LION BRAND® Fun Fur
Bulky Weight Yarn [1¾ ounces, 64 yards
(50 grams, 58 meters) per ball]
2 balls #144 Lavender (B)
or color of your choice
LION BRAND® Fancy Fur
Super Bulky Weight Yarn [1¾ ounces, 39 yards
(50 grams, 35 meters) per ball]
2 balls #295 Party Pink (D)
or color of your choice
LION BRAND crochet hook size N-13 [9 mm]
or size needed for gauge
LION BRAND large-eyed blunt needle

GAUGE

10 sc and 13 rows = 4" [10 cm] with A

■ CAT MAT

With A, ch 39.

Row 1: With A, sc in 2nd ch from hook and in each ch across: 38 sc.

Rows 2-5: With A, ch 1, turn, sc in each sc across. Fasten off A. Holding 2 strands of B together, join B.

Rows 6 and 7: With 2 strands of B held together, ch 1, turn, sc in each sc across. Fasten off both strands of B and join C.

Rows 8-10: With C, ch 1, turn, sc in each sc across. Fasten off C and join D.

Rows 11-13: With D, ch 1, turn, sc in each sc across. Fasten off D and join A.

Row 14: With A, ch 1, turn, sc in each sc across.

Rows 15-53: Repeat Rows 2-14 three more times.

Rows 54-62: Repeat Rows 2-10 once. Do not fasten off C at end of last row.

Row 63: With C, ch 1, turn, slip stitch in each sc across. Fasten off.

■ FINISHING

Weave in ends.

DOG MAT

Finished Size: 22" x 30" [56 x 76 cm]

MATERIALS

LION BRAND® Wool-Ease®
Worsted Weight Yarn [3 ounces, 197 yards
(85 grams, 180 meters) per ball]
1 ball #174 Avocado (A)
1 ball #148 Turquoise (C)
or colors of your choice
LION BRAND® Fun Fur
Bulky Weight Yarn [1¾ ounces, 64 yards
(50 grams, 58 meters) per ball]
3 balls #194 Lime (B)
or color of your choice
LION BRAND® Fancy Fur
Super Bulky Weight Yarn [1¾ ounces, 39 yards
(50 grams, 35 meters) per ball]
2 balls #257 Stormy Sea (D)
or color of your choice
LION BRAND crochet hook size N-13 [9 mm]
or size needed for gauge
LION BRAND large-eyed blunt needle

GAUGE
10 sc and 13 rows = 4" [10 cm] with A

■ DOG MAT
With A, ch 56.

Row 1: With A, sc in 2nd ch from hook and in each ch across: 55 sc.

Rows 2-5: With A, ch 1, turn, sc in each sc across. Fasten off A. Holding 2 strands of B together, join B.

Rows 6 and 7: With 2 strands of B held together, ch 1, turn, sc in each sc across. Fasten off both strands of B and join C.

Rows 8-10: With C, ch 1, turn, sc in each sc across. Fasten off C and join D.

Rows 11-13: With D, ch 1, turn, sc in each sc across. Fasten off D and join A.

Row 14: With A, ch 1, turn, sc in each sc across.

Rows 15-92: Repeat Rows 2-14 six more times.

Rows 93-96: Repeat Rows 2-5. Do not fasten off A at end of last row.

Row 97: With A, ch 1, turn, slip stitch in each sc across. Fasten off.

■ FINISHING
Weave in ends.

23

NECKWARMER

DESIGNER: **ANNEMARIE LAWSON**

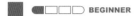

BEGINNER

Finished Circumference: 26" [66 cm]
Finished Length: 12" [30.5 cm]

MATERIALS

LION BRAND® Lion® Bouclé ![SUPER BULKY 6]
Super Bulky Weight Yarn [2½ ounces, 57 yards
(70 grams, 52 meters) per ball]
2 balls #112 Rose (A)
or color of your choice
LION BRAND® Jiffy® ![BULKY 5]
Bulky Weight Yarn [3 ounces, 135 yards
(85 grams, 123 meters) per ball]
1 ball #195 Dusty Pink (B)
or color of your choice
LION BRAND Speed Hook (size 35/19 mm)
or size needed for gauge
LION BRAND large-eyed blunt needle
LION BRAND split ring marker

GAUGE

8 half double crochet and 7 rows = 7" [18 cm] with
1 strand each of A and B held together

Note: Neckwarmer is crocheted with 1 strand each
of A and B held together throughout.

NECKWARMER

With 1 strand each of A and B held together, chain
29; join with a slip stitch in first chain to form a ring,
being careful not to twist the stitches.

Round 1: Chain 1, half double crochet in each chain around; do not
join: 29 half double crochet.

Note: Work in continuous rounds. Do not turn and do not join
rounds. Place marker to indicate beginning of round. Move marker up
each round.

Round 2: Half double crochet in each half double crochet around.

Repeat Round 2 until piece measures 12" [30.5 cm] from beginning.
Fasten off.

FINISHING

Weave in ends.

Blues Dishcloth

 BEGINNER

Finished Size: 10" x 10" [25.5 x 25.5 cm]

MATERIALS

LION BRAND® Lion® Cotton
Worsted Weight Yarn [5 ounces, 236 yards
(140 grams, 212 meters) per ball]
1 ball #110 Navy (A)
1 ball #108 Morning Glory Blue (B)
1 ball #183 Periwinkle (C)
1 ball #148 Turquoise (D)
or colors of your choice
LION BRAND crochet hook size E-4 [3.5 mm]
or size needed for gauge
LION BRAND large-eyed blunt needle

GAUGE

13$\frac{1}{2}$ single crochet = 4" [10 cm]

■ DISHCLOTH

With A, chain 21.

Row 1: Single crochet in 2nd chain from hook
and in each chain across: 20 single crochet.

Row 2: Chain 1, turn, single crochet in each
single crochet across.

Repeat Row 2 until piece measures 6" [15 cm]
from beginning. Fasten off A and join B.

Striped Border

Row 1: With B, single crochet in next 19 single crochet across row,
work 3 single crochet in last single crochet for corner; turn to work
across ends of rows and work 19 single crochet evenly spaced along
side of piece.

Rows 2-5: Chain 1, turn, single crochet in each single crochet along
side; work 3 single crochet in corner; single crochet in each single
crochet across the top. At end of Row 5, fasten off B and join C.

Rows 6-10: With C, repeat Row 2. At end of Row 10, fasten off C and
join D.

Rows 11-15: With D, repeat Row 2. At end of Row 15, fasten off.

■ FINISHING

Weave in ends.

GREENS DISHCLOTH

 BEGINNER

Finished Size: 10" x 10" [25.5 x 25.5 cm]

MATERIALS
LION BRAND® Lion® Cotton MEDIUM 4
Worsted Weight Yarn [5 ounces, 236 yards
(140 grams, 212 meters) per ball]
1 ball #123 Seaspray (A)
1 ball #181 Sage (B)
1 ball #131 Fern Green (C)
or colors of your choice
LION BRAND crochet hook size E-4 [3.5 mm]
or size needed for gauge
LION BRAND large-eyed blunt needle

GAUGE
13½ single crochet = 4" [10 cm]

■ DISHCLOTH
With A, chain 21.

Row 1: Single crochet in 2nd chain from hook
and in each chain across: 20 single crochet.

Row 2: Chain 1, turn, single crochet in each
single crochet across.

Repeat Row 2 until piece measures 6" [15 cm]
from beginning. Fasten off A and join B.

Striped Border
Row 1: With B, single crochet in next 19 single crochet across row,
work 3 single crochet in last single crochet for corner; turn to work
across ends of rows and work 19 single crochet evenly spaced along
side of piece.

Rows 2-5: Chain 1, turn, single crochet in each single crochet along
side; work 3 single crochet in corner; single crochet in each single
crochet across the top. At end of Row 5, fasten off B and join C.

Rows 6-10: With C, repeat Row 2. At end of Row 10, fasten off C and
join A.

Rows 11-15: With A, repeat Row 2. At end of Row 15, fasten off.

■ FINISHING
Weave in ends.

PINKS DISHCLOTH

▣ ◖☐☐☐☐ **BEGINNER**

Finished Size: 10" x 10" [25.5 x 25.5 cm]

MATERIALS

LION BRAND® Lion® Cotton **MEDIUM 4**
  Worsted Weight Yarn [5 ounces, 236 yards
  (140 grams, 212 meters) per ball]
  1 ball #112 Poppy Red (A)
  1 ball #140 Rose (B)
  or colors of your choice
LION BRAND crochet hook size E-4 [3.5 mm]
  or size needed for gauge
LION BRAND large-eyed blunt needle

GAUGE

13½ single crochet = 4" [10 cm]

▣ DISHCLOTH

With A, chain 21.

Row 1: Single crochet in 2nd chain from hook
and in each chain across: 20 single crochet.

Row 2: Chain 1, turn, single crochet in each
single crochet across.

Repeat Row 2 until piece measures 6" [15 cm]
from beginning. Fasten off A and join B.

Striped Border

Row 1: With B, single crochet in next 19 single crochet across row,
work 3 single crochet in last single crochet for corner; turn to work
across ends of rows and work 19 single crochet evenly spaced along
side of piece.

Rows 2-5: Chain 1, turn, single crochet in each single crochet along
side; work 3 single crochet in corner; single crochet in each single
crochet across the top. At end of Row 5, fasten off B and join A.

Rows 6-10: With A, repeat Row 2. At end of Row 10, fasten off A
and join B.

Rows 11-15: With B, repeat Row 2. At end of Row 15, fasten off.

▣ FINISHING

Weave in ends.

Bath Mitt

DESIGNER: **KIM KOTARY**

BEGINNER

Finished Size: 5" x 8" [12.5 x 20.5 cm]

MATERIALS

LION BRAND® Lion® Cotton
Worsted Weight Yarn [5 ounces, 236 yards
(140 grams, 212 meters) per ball]
1 ball #123 Seaspray
or color of your choice
LION BRAND crochet hook size E-4 [3.5 mm]
or size needed for gauge
LION BRAND large-eyed blunt needle

GAUGE

14 single crochet and 17 rows = 4" [10 cm]

MITT

Chain 18.

Row 1: Single crochet in 2nd chain from hook and in each chain across: 17 single crochet.

Row 2: Ch 1, turn, single crochet in each single crochet across.

Repeat Row 2 until piece measures 16" [40.5 cm]. Do not fasten off.

FINISHING

Fold piece in half, bringing last row up to meet first row. Turn work and single crochet through both layers to join along one side of Mitt. Fasten off.

From RS, join yarn to remaining side at fold. Single crochet through both layers to join. At top edge of Mitt, chain 11. Turn, single crochet in 2nd chain from hook and in each chain, slip stitch in beginning st to make hanging loop. Fasten off.

Weave in ends.

SINGLE CROCHET WASHCLOTH

 BEGINNER

Finished Size: 9" x 9" [23 x 23 cm]

MATERIALS

LION BRAND® Lion® Cotton
Worsted Weight Yarn [5 ounces, 236 yards
(140 grams, 212 meters) per ball]
1 ball #183 Periwinkle
or color of your choice
LION BRAND crochet hook size E-4 [3.5 mm]
or size needed for gauge
LION BRAND large-eyed blunt needle

GAUGE

15 single crochet = 4" [10 cm]

■ WASHCLOTH

Chain 35.

Row 1: Single crochet in 2nd chain from hook and in each chain across: 34 single crochet.

Row 2: Chain 1, turn, single crochet in each single crochet across.

Repeat Row 2 until piece measures 9" [23 cm] from beginning. Fasten off.

■ FINISHING

Weave in ends.

HALF DOUBLE CROCHET WASHCLOTH

DESIGNER: **KIM KOTARY**

◧◩□□ BEGINNER

Finished Size: 9" x 9" [23 x 23 cm]

MATERIALS
LION BRAND® Lion® Cotton **MEDIUM 4**
Worsted Weight Yarn [5 ounces, 236 yards
(140 grams, 212 meters) per ball]
1 ball #144 Grape
or color of your choice
LION BRAND crochet hook size E-4 [3.5 mm]
or size needed for gauge
LION BRAND large-eyed blunt needle

GAUGE
15 half double crochet = 4" [10 cm]

■ WASHCLOTH
Chain 36.

Row 1: Half double crochet in 3rd chain from hook and in each chain across: 34 half double crochet.

Row 2: Chain 2, turn, half double crochet in each half double crochet across.

Repeat Row 2 until piece measures 9" [23 cm] from beginning. Fasten off.

■ FINISHING
Weave in ends.

DOUBLE CROCHET WASHCLOTH

DESIGNER: **KIM KOTARY**

◧□□□ BEGINNER

Finished Size: 9" x 9" [23 x 23 cm]

MATERIALS
LION BRAND® Lion® Cotton **MEDIUM 4**
Worsted Weight Yarn [5 ounces, 236 yards
(140 grams, 212 meters) per ball]
1 ball #098 Natural
or color of your choice
LION BRAND crochet hook size E-4 [3.5 mm]
or size needed for gauge
LION BRAND large-eyed blunt needle

GAUGE
15 double crochet = 4" [10 cm]

■ WASHCLOTH
Chain 37.

Row 1: Double crochet in 4th chain from hook and in each chain across: 34 double crochet.

Row 2: Chain 3, turn, double crochet in each double crochet across.

Repeat Row 2 until piece measures 9" [23 cm] from beginning. Fasten off.

■ FINISHING
Weave in ends.

POCKET MARKET BAG

● □ □ □ **BEGINNER**

Finished Size: 10" x 13" [25.5 x 33 cm] not including handles

MATERIALS

LION BRAND® Cotton-Ease 【4】 MEDIUM
  Worsted Weight Yarn [3½ ounces, 207 yards (100 grams, 188 meters) per ball]
  2 balls #122 Taupe (A)
  1 ball #186 Maize (B)
  or colors of your choice
LION BRAND crochet hook size G-6 [4.25 mm] or size needed for gauge
LION BRAND large-eyed blunt needle

GAUGE

14 single crochet and 16 rows = 4" [10 cm]

■ FRONT

With A, chain 36.

Row 1: Single crochet in 2nd chain from hook and each chain across: 35 single crochet.

Row 2: Chain 1, turn, single crochet in each single crochet across.

Repeat Row 2 until piece measures 13" [33 cm] from beginning. Fasten off.

■ BACK

Work same as Front.

■ HANDLE
(make 2)

With A, chain 51.

Row 1: Single crochet in 2nd chain from hook and each chain across: 50 single crochet.

Rows 2-5: Chain 1, turn, single crochet in each single crochet across. Fasten off.

■ POCKET

With B, chain 29.

Row 1: Single crochet in 2nd chain from hook and each chain across: 28 single crochet.

Row 2: Chain 1, turn, single crochet in each single crochet across.

Repeat Row 2 until piece measures 5" [12.5 cm]. Fasten off.

■ SMALL FLOWER

Ch 6; join with slip st to form ring.

Rnd 1: Ch 1, [sc, ch 4] 8 times in ring; join with slip st in first sc: 8 ch-4 loops.

Rnd 2: Working behind ch-4 loops in Rnd 1, ch 1, *sc in ring between next 2 sc, ch 5; repeat from * around; join with slip st in first sc: 8 ch-5 spaces.
Fasten off. Weave in ends.

■ MEDIUM FLOWER
(make 2)

Ch 5; join with sl st to form ring.

Rnd 1: (Ch 5, sl st) 7 times in ring; join with slip st in first slip st: 7 ch-5 loops.

Rnd 2: Working behind Rnd 1, ch 1, sc in ring between next 2 sl st, (ch 2, sc in next space) 6 times, ch 2; join with sl st in top of first sc: 7 sc.

Rnd 3: (Ch 5, sl st in same sc, ch 5, sl st in next ch-2 space, ch 5, sl st in next sc) 7 times: 21 ch-5 loops.
Fasten off. Weave in ends.

■ FINISHING

Sew Pocket to Front, 10 rows above lower edge.

From right side, work single crochet evenly spaced through both layers to join Front and Back of Bag, leaving top open. Sew Handles to wrong side of bag 1" [2.5 cm] from each side. Weave in ends.

Using photo as a guide, sew flowers to bag.

SHRUG

 **BEGINNER**

Finished Sizes: S/M (L, 1X/2X)
Finished Cross Back (Shoulder to Shoulder): 20 (24, 28)"
[51 (61, 71) cm]

Note: Pattern is written for smallest size with changes for larger sizes in parentheses. When only one number is given, it applies to all sizes. To follow pattern more easily, circle all numbers pertaining to your size before beginning.

MATERIALS

LION BRAND® Homespun®
Bulky Weight Yarn [6 ounces, 185 yards
(170 grams, 169 meters) per skein]
3 skeins #397 Russet
or color of your choice
LION BRAND crochet hook size K-10.5 [6.5 mm]
LION BRAND large-eyed blunt needle

GAUGE

10 double crochet and 5 rows = 4" [10 cm]

■ SHRUG

Chain 52 (55, 58).

Row 1: Double crochet in 4th chain from hook and in each chain across: 50 (53, 56) double crochet (3 skipped chains at beginning count as 1 double crochet).

Row 2: Chain 3, turn, double crochet in next double crochet and in each double crochet across.

Repeat Row 2 until piece measures 44 (50, 56)" [112 (127, 142) cm] from beginning. Fasten off.

■ FINISHING

Fold Shrug lengthwise. Sew ends together for 12 (13, 14)" [30.5 (33, 35.5) cm]. Leave center 20 (24, 28)" [51 (61, 71) cm] open for body.

Wrist Drawstring (make 2)

Chain 90. Fasten off. Thread a Drawstring through stitches just above wrist.

Neck Drawstring

Chain 160. Fasten off. Thread Drawstring through stitches at back of neck, pull ends to gather, then tie into a bow.

Granny Square Baby Afghan

DESIGNER: **MOLLY BETTRIDGE**

INTERMEDIATE

Finished Size: 24" x 36" [61 x 91.5 cm]

MATERIALS

LION BRAND® Babysoft®
Sport Weight Yarn [Solids: 5 ounces,
459 yards (140 grams, 420 meters);
Prints: 4 ounces, 367 yards (113 grams,
335 meters) per ball]
1 ball #268 Carousel Print (A)
1 ball #176 Spring Green (B)
or colors of your choice
LION BRAND crochet hook size E-4 [3.5 mm]
or size needed for gauge
LION BRAND large-eyed blunt needle

GAUGE

Full square = 3½" [9 cm] square

■ AFGHAN

■ FULL SQUARE
(make 24 with A and 15 with B)

Ch 6; join with sl st in beg ch to form a ring.

Rnd 1: Ch 3 (counts as a dc), 2 dc in ring, ch 1 (3 dc in ring, ch 1) 3 times; join with sl st in top of beg ch: 12 dc.

Rnd 2: Ch 3 (counts as a dc), dc in next 2 dc, *(2 dc, ch 1, 2 dc) in ch-sp, dc in next 3 dc; rep from * 2 more times, (2 dc, ch 1, 2 dc) in last ch-sp; join with sl st in top of beg ch: 28 dc.

Rnd 3: Ch 3 (counts as a dc), dc in next 4 dc, *(2 dc, ch 1, 2 dc) in ch-sp, dc in next 7 dc; rep from * 2 more times, (2 dc, ch 1, 2 dc) in last ch-sp, dc in last 2 dc; join with sl st in top of beg ch: 44 dc.

Rnd 4: Ch 3 (counts as a dc), dc in next 6 dc, *(2 dc, ch 1, 2 dc) in ch-sp, dc in next 11 dc; rep from * 2 more times, (2 dc, ch 1, 2 dc) in last ch-sp, dc in last 4 dc; join with sl st in top of beg ch: 60 dc.

■ HALF SQUARE
(make 16 with B)

Ch 4; join with sl st in beg ch to form a ring.

Row 1: Ch 3 (counts as a dc), 2 dc in ring, ch 1, 3 dc in ring: 6 dc.

Row 2: Ch 3 (counts as a dc), turn, dc in first dc, 2 dc in next dc, dc in next dc, (2 dc, ch 1, 2 dc) in ch-sp, dc in next dc, 2 dc in next dc, 2 dc in top of t-ch: 14 dc.

Row 3: Ch 3 (counts as a dc), turn, dc in first dc, 2 dc in next dc, dc in next 5 dc, (2 dc, ch 1, 2 dc) in ch-sp, dc in next 5 dc, 2 dc in next dc, 2 dc in t-ch: 22 dc.

Row 4: Ch 3 (counts as a dc), turn, dc in first dc, 2 dc in next dc, dc in next 9 dc, (2 dc, ch 1, 2 dc) in ch-sp, dc in next 9 dc, 2 dc in next dc, 2 dc in top of t-ch: 30 dc.

■ CORNER SQUARE
(make 4 with B)

Ch 4; join with sl st in beg ch to form a ring.

Row 1: Ch 3 (counts as a dc), 4 dc in ring.

Row 2: Ch 3 (counts as a dc), turn, dc in first dc, dc in next 3 dc, 2 dc in top of t-ch: 7 dc.

Row 3: Ch 3 (counts as a dc), turn, dc in first dc, 2 dc in next dc, dc in next 3 dc, 2 dc in next dc, 2 dc in top of t-ch: 11 dc.

Row 4: Ch 3 (counts as a dc), turn, dc in first dc, dc in next dc, dc in next 7 dc, 2 dc in next dc, 2 dc in top of t-ch: 15 dc.

■ FINISHING

Following diagram, sew squares together.

Edging: From right side, join B in any dc, ch 1, work sc evenly spaced around, working 3 sc in each corner; join with sl st in first sc. Work 1 more rnd in sc, working 3 sc in each corner. Fasten off. Weave in ends.

Assembly Diagram

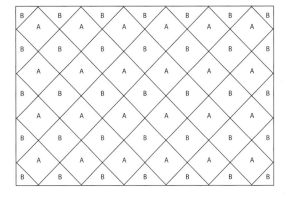

More Knit and Crochet leaflets featuring
Lion Brand® Yarn!

Leaflet 4059

Leaflet 4165

Leaflet 4687

Leaflet 4686

Leaflet 4376

Leaflet 4375

Leaflet 4374

Leaflet 3985

Leaflet 3984

Leaflet 3982

Leaflet 4056

Leaflet 4688

Look for these titles and more at your retailer or visit **www.leisurearts.com**.